KU-341-287

TEUTONIC KNIGHT

🥄 A HORRIBLE DEATH

Henry is believed to have contracted leprosy, or a similar debilitating disease, in 1406. Plagued by constant illness, he died of a seizure in 1413 aged just 46. A prophecy had foretold that he would die in Jerusalem. In fact, he died in the Jerusalem Chapel in Westminster Abbey.

💧 BATTLE OF SHREWSBURY

Henry's reign was plagued by rebellions. Most notable of these was the revolt led by his once loyal supporters, the Percys, Dukes of Northumberland. On 21st July 1403 Henry Percy, known as Harry Hotspur, was defeated at the Battle of Shrewsbury.

LONDON'S GUILDHALL

Guilds were professional or craft associations formed by merchants and traders in medieval towns to protect their mutual interests. They built magnificent guildhalls from where they conducted their business, which also often became the centres of local government. Probably the finest guildhall was built in London between 1411-26.

As a young man Henry travelled widely, throughout Europe and the Middle East, fighting alongside the Teutonic Knights, an order of religious knights who fought in the crusades, in Lithuania. He made a pilgrimage to Jerusalem and promised to return on a crusade himself, though he never did.

JOAN OF NAVARRE

Henry married Mary de Bohun in 1380, who bore him seven children, including the future king, Henry V. Following her death he married Joan of Navarre, in 1403, whose effigy can be seen above their canopied tomb in Canterbury Cathedral. Navarre was an independent kingdom on the French and Spanish borders.

EMPEROR MANUEL II

In 1402 Henry received Manuel II, the Byzantine emperor, at court on a state visit to England. The Byzantine empire grew out of what was the Eastern Roman Empire when that collapsed in the 5th century. Occupying much of what is now known as the Middle East, Byzantium resisted invasion from the feudal states of Europe until the early 14th century, when it fell to the Ottoman Turks.

1403	up independent	1405	1406
Percy rebels defeated by Henry at Battle of Shrewsbury.	Welsh Parliament.	Second Percy rebellion.	Henry IV contracts leprosy.
	1404	1405	1408
1404	Welsh form allegiance with French against English.	French send an army to help Welsh revolt against English.	Third Percy rebellion.
Owain Glyndwr sets			1413
			Henry IV dies.

⚔ GOVERNMENT   🥄 HEALTH & MEDICINE   ⚖ JUSTICE   ✝ RELIGION   📖 SCIENCE

MONMOUTH CASTLE

Monmouth Castle was first built between 1067-71 during the Norman invasion of Wales and greatly extended later, principally during the reign of Edward I, when a fortified bridge and town wall were added. The castle was the birthplace, in 1387, of Henry V.

THE CAMBRIDGE PLOT

In 1415 a plot was uncovered to remove Henry from the throne in favour of his cousin Edmund Mortimer who, as Richard II's heir, had a stronger claim to the crown. Known as the Cambridge Plot, it was unsuccessful and the ringleaders were brought to trial for treason.

HENRY V

BORN 1387 • ACCEDED 1413 • DIED 1422

ne of the first acts by Henry on becoming king in 1413, at the age of 25, was to renew Edward III's claim to the French throne. The war with France that followed served the dual purpose of extending his military prowess and in unifying a divided nobility against a common enemy. A zealous and religious man, Henry was also a scholar and a patron of the arts who might have gone down in history as one of our greatest monarchs but for his untimely and premature death at the age of 35.

PREMATURE DEATH

Always a healthy, robust young man, Henry died somewhat prematurely during his French campaign. He contracted dysentery and died at Vincennes Castle on 1st September 1422. Had he lived just a few weeks longer he would have inherited the French throne, for Charles VI followed him to the grave less than two months later. Henry is shown here being married to Katherine of France, Charles' sister.

R: DE: FRANCE: h: LE: CINQVIESHE:

THE BATTLE OF AGINCOURT

One of the greatest and best remembered battles of the Middle Ages was fought at Agincourt (left), in France, during the 100 Years' War. On 25th October 1415 Henry led an English force of just 9000 men, one-third the size of the opposing French army. The French relied on cavalry, but they became bogged down in heavy mud and fell to the mercy of the English archers. About 7000 Frenchmen lost their lives, compared to just 400 English.

SHAKESPEARE'S HERO

The popular image of Henry V as a saintly hero king is largely an invention of Shakespeare. The Tudor monarchs were descended from the House of Lancaster and it suited their purpose to make heroes of their ancestors. While unquestionably a brave and able soldier, many contemporary chroniclers portray him as arrogant and manipulative.

HEIR TO THE FRENCH THRONE

At the 'Treaty of Troyes', in 1420, Henry forced the French king, Charles VI (considered by many to be mad), to make him his heir and regent of France. He also requested the hand of Charles's daughter, Katherine, in marriage. They were married later the same year, thus briefly uniting the crowns of England and France.

WELSH REVOLT

The Welsh revolt against English rule, led by Owain Glyndwr, was largely dealt with by Henry, as Prince of Wales, during his father's reign, though he never succeeded in finally defeating the Welsh. The revolt diffused itself on the death of Glyndwr in 1416, but the young Henry cut his military teeth on the Welsh campaigns and learned the art of tactics against superior odds.

WAR WITH FRANCE

A brilliant soldier and tactician, Henry took advantage of the weakened state of the French monarchy, damaged by corrupt government and civil war. He won several resounding victories and recaptured Normandy and parts of Aquitaine. The victories were largely made possible by the skill of the English archers. If captured, the French cut off their fore and middle fingers to prevent them from drawing bows again. Before battle it became the practice for archers to wave their two fingers in a V-sign as a gesture of defiance, a derisive gesture still used today.

1413 *Henry V succeeds his father to the throne.* **1415** *The Cambridge Plot (an attempt to depose Henry and*	*replace him with his cousin, Edmund Mortimer, Earl of March) is put down by Henry.* **1415** *Henry declares war on*	*France and makes claim for French throne.* **1415** *English defeat French at the Battle of Agincourt, against massive odds.*	**1420** *Treaty of Troyes; Henry becomes Regent of France and heir to French throne.* **1420** *Henry marries Katherine,*	*daughter of Charles VI of France.* **1422** *Henry V dies of dysentery in France just 2 months before succeeding to the French throne.*

5

GOVERNMENT   HEALTH & MEDICINE   JUSTICE   RELIGION   SCIENCE

BOY KING

Henry was just 10 months old when he succeeded first, to the English throne on the death of his father in 1422, and then to the French throne on the death of his grandfather, Charles VI, two months later. During his minority Humphrey, Duke of Gloucester, was appointed Regent of England and John, Duke of Bedford, Regent of France. Henry took over governance himself at the age of 15 in 1437.

HENRY VI

BORN 1421 • ACCEDED 1422 • DEPOSED 1461
RESTORED 1470 • DEPOSED 1471 • DIED 1471

In less warlike times Henry VI might have become one of our better kings, but he was ill-equipped to deal with the violence and bitter political quarrels of his time. A gentle, well-educated and devoutly religious man, he had a naive, almost unworldly nature. This simplicity was seen as weakness by his enemies, who ruthlessly exploited him. His reign was plagued by civil war, eventually resulting in his deposition and murder in 1471 at the age of 49.

MENTAL ILLNESS

Throughout his life Henry suffered from recurring bouts of mental illness, inherited from his maternal grandfather. The first attack came at the age of 32, in 1454, and his cousin Richard, Duke of York, was made Protector of England during his incapacitation.

JOAN OF ARC
(1412-31)

Born to a peasant family in Domrémy, France, Joan of Arc began (in 1429) the revolt against Henry VI that eventually led to the expulsion of the English from France, claiming her inspiration in a vision from God. Captured by the English in 1431 she was burned at the stake in Rouen, though the French continued the fight in her name. In 1920 she was canonised by Pope Benedict XV.

1422
Henry VI succeeds his father to the throne.
1422
Henry VI becomes king of France on the death
of his grandfather.
1422
During Henry's minority, John, Duke of Bedford, appointed Regent of

 ARCHITECTURE   ARTS & LITERATURE   EXPLORATION   FAMOUS BATTLE

PATRON OF LEARNING

Henry was a quiet, learned man, who encouraged others to study by founding the King's College of Our Lady at Eton (left) in 1440. The following year he founded King's College at Cambridge University to receive its scholars.

WARS OF THE ROSES

In 1455 Richard, Duke of York, who had been instated as Protector during Henry's mental illness, was dismissed. He rebelled against Henry and assumed control of the government, marking the beginning of the 'Wars of the Roses' (see pages 14-15), a dynastic struggle for the English throne.

END OF THE 100 YEARS' WAR

The 100 Years' War with France, begun in 1337 by Edward III when asserting his claim to the French throne, came to an end in 1453 when the English were finally driven out of France. All of England's possessions in France, with the exception of Calais, were lost.

THE KING IS DEPOSED

The civil war that resulted from Richard, Duke of York's dismissal as Protector eventually led, in 1461, to Henry being deposed because of his ineffectual rule. He was replaced on the throne by Richard's son, who ruled as Edward IV until 1470, when Henry was briefly reinstated as king before being overthrown again the following year by Edward.

MURDERED IN THE TOWER

At the Battle of Tewkesbury, in May 1471, during the Wars of the Roses, Henry and his Queen, Margaret, were captured and his son Edward killed. Imprisoned in the Tower of London, he was officially found dead in bed one morning a few weeks later, but it is believed he was murdered while at prayer.

MARGARET OF ANJOU

Henry married Margaret of Anjou in 1445. Known as the 'she-wolf of France', she was quite ruthless and completely dominated the king, particularly during his bouts of mental illness. She stoutly supported the Lancashire cause in the Wars of the Roses and was imprisoned following the Battle of Tewkesbury in 1471. She was released five years later, on payment of a ransom by the French king, and died at Anjou, her homeland, in 1482.

France, and Humphrey, Duke of Gloucester, as Regent of England.

1429
Joan of Arc expels English from France.

1431
Joan of Arc burnt at stake by English.

1437
Henry VI assumes government of England

from his Regent.

1453
End of 100 Years' War - England loses all French possessions, except Calais.

1454
Henry VI suffers bout of mental illness.

1454
Richard, Duke of York, made Protector

during king's illness.

1455
Duke of York rebels against king and assumes control of government.

GOVERNMENT   HEALTH & MEDICINE   JUSTICE   RELIGION   SCIENCE

EDWARD IV
BORN 1442 • ACCEDED 1461 • DEPOSED 1470
RESTORED 1471 • DIED 1483

When Edward IV came to the throne in 1461 after defeating Henry VI at the Battle of Towton, in Yorkshire, he was just 19 years old. He was said to be a giant of a man, about 6ft. 3ins. tall when the average height was just 5ft. 4ins. He began his reign as a genial, well-mannered diplomat, but when he died at the age of 40 he was accused of living a life of debauchery and excess.

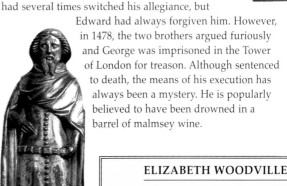

DUKE OF CLARENCE

Edward's brother George, Duke of Clarence, had several times switched his allegiance, but Edward had always forgiven him. However, in 1478, the two brothers argued furiously and George was imprisoned in the Tower of London for treason. Although sentenced to death, the means of his execution has always been a mystery. He is popularly believed to have been drowned in a barrel of malmsey wine.

THE RIGHTFUL SUCCESSOR

Edward is generally considered to have had a stronger claim to the throne than Henry VI. His grandfather was the son of Edward III's 5th son, Edmund, and his grandmother was descended from Edward III's 3rd son, Lionel. Henry VI, on the other hand, was only descended from Edward III's 4th son, John of Gaunt.

ELIZABETH WOODVILLE

Edward married Elizabeth Woodville in 1464 and she bore him 10 children. She was the widow of a commoner, which sparked off the rift between Edward and his cousin Richard, Earl of Warwick, who feared his position at court might be undermined.

1455	1455	1460	1461	1470
Start of the Wars of the Roses.	First printed Bible published in Germany.	Henry VI captured and his wife escapes to Scotland.	Edward, Duke of York, crowned king as Edward IV.	Edward driven into exile by Henry VI's supporters.
1455 The Duke of York defeats Henry at the Battle of St. Albans.	1460 Battle of Northampton.	1461 Henry VI is deposed.	1464 Edward marries Elizabeth Woodville.	1470-71 Warwick is banished and Henry reinstated to thron

 ARCHITECTURE   📖 ARTS & LITERATURE   ↳ EXPLORATION   💣 FAMOUS BATTLES

WILLIAM CAXTON

The first printing press in England was set up by William Caxton in 1476 (left). The wooden hand-press was modelled on wine presses used in the Rhine valley and remained in use, with only minor changes, for over 350 years. Caxton, a wool merchant by trade, learned the craft of printing in Europe and he produced over 18,000 pages before he died in 1491. Books had previously to be produced by hand, which made them very expensive. Printing made books available to an ever-more literate public at reasonable cost.

COURT OF REQUESTS

Edward was a very able administrator and introduced several legal reforms, the most notable of which was the Court of Requests, where poor tenants could take complaints against greedy landlords and ask the officials to adjudicate a fair rent.

✝ ST. GEORGE'S CHAPEL

Edward built the magnificent St. George's Chapel at Windsor Castle to rival Henry VI's chapel at Eton, which could be clearly seen from the royal castle. St. George's is perhaps the finest piece of late medieval church architecture in Europe, with breath-takingly beautiful fan vaulting in the Perpendicular style.

BATTLE OF BARNET

The Battle of Barnet (below) was fought in Hertfordshire between the forces of Edward and Henry VI on Easter Day, 14th April 1471. Edward had recently returned from exile in Flanders to reassert his claim to the throne. Richard, Earl of Warwick, was killed in the battle.

INCREASED TRADE

Edward was determined to end the dreadful civil wars that had raged in England during the reign of Henry VI and restore peace and economic stability. He did a great deal to help English merchants, particularly those involved in the wool trade. England enjoyed the greatest period of prosperity this country had ever witnessed, which made him very popular with businessmen.

EXILE IN FLANDERS

In 1470 Richard, Earl of Warwick, known as 'the Kingmaker', who had earlier helped Edward onto the throne, switched his allegiance to Henry VI. Edward was forced to flee the country, to exile in Flanders, and Warwick helped Henry VI return to the throne, briefly.

1471 *Henry captured at Battle of Tewkesbury.*	*Battle of Barnet.* **1471** *Henry VI is murdered.*	**1478** *Spanish Inquisition established.*
1471 *arwick, 'the Kingmaker', defeated and killed at*	**1471** *Edward IV, returns from exile and is proclaimed king again.*	**1483** *Edward IV dies.*

EDWARD V

BORN 1470 • ACCEDED 1483 • DIED 1483(?)

EDWARD DECLARED ILLEGITIMATE

In June 1483 Parliament declared Edward V (and his brother) illegitimate and deposed him in favour of his uncle, who became Richard III. Apparently, Edward IV had already been betrothed to another at the time of his marriage to Elizabeth Woodville. Under medieval law, a betrothal carried legal status and so the marriage was declared invalid.

LUDLOW CASTLE

Edward and his brother Richard lived at Ludlow Castle, in Shropshire, from 1472 until the untimely death of their father in 1483. Ludlow Castle began as a simple Norman stronghold in about 1085. It was substantially enlarged in the 12th and 13th centuries, when it acquired an unusual circular chapel. It became royal property in 1461 when Edward Mortimer, its then owner, was crowned king as Edward IV.

When Edward IV died in 1483 the throne passed to his eldest son Edward, who was then just 13 years old. Edward's uncle Richard, Duke of Gloucester, was appointed Protector during the king's minority, according to the provisions of Edward IV's will. When both his nephews were afterwards declared illegitimate, Richard was invited by Parliament to become king as Edward IV's brother, and therefore the rightful heir. The later disappearance of the two princes is one of history's greatest mysteries.

THE PRINCES MURDERED

The last recorded sighting of the two princes was in September, in the palace gardens. They are believed to have been suffocated, by unknown assailants, in the Bloody Tower, so named after the deed. Two children's bodies were discovered at the Tower in 1674 and subsequently buried in Westminster Abbey, but forensic examination in 1933 failed to prove they were the skeletons of the princes.

1483
Edward V accedes to the throne.
1483
Richard of Gloucester (Edward's uncle) becomes

Protector of England.
1483
Edward V declared illegitimate and imprisoned in the Tower, with his brother Richard.

1483
Edward and his younger brother, Richard, believed to have been murdered in the Tower.

🏛 ARCHITECTURE   📖 ARTS & LITERATURE   🗺 EXPLORATION   ⚫ FAMOUS BATTLE

THE CASE AGAINST RICHARD III

Richard III has always been the prime suspect as being responsible for murdering the princes, though he was never accused of it in his lifetime. The accusations came later. It could be argued that, as parliament had already been convinced of their illegitimacy they were no longer a threat to his crown, so why bother murdering them? It could equally be argued, of course, that their murders removed any threats there might have been. If Richard was responsible he covered his tracks well, and today the only 'evidence' of any kind against him is in the words of Shakespeare's plays, which are largely works of fiction based loosely on fact and biased towards the Tudor propaganda machine.

THE CASE AGAINST HENRY VII

The dynastic struggle for supremacy, known as the 'Wars of the Roses', came to a head in 1485, at the Battle of Bosworth Field. The victor, Henry Tudor, who became Henry VII, defeated and killed Richard III, thus removing any further threat to the crown. Henry's claim to the throne was less valid than Richard's and so in order to make himself more acceptable as king he set about a character assassination of Richard III. It was he who first started the rumour that Richard had murdered his nephews, though he had as much, if not more, to gain by killing all Yorkist claimants to the throne, including Richard himself.

ONE OF HISTORY'S GREAT MYSTERIES

Despite the finger of suspicion having been firmly pointed at Richard III for the princes' murders, no evidence has ever come to light. No bodies have ever been proved to be the princes, so they may not have been murdered at all, but forced into hiding, particularly after the Tudor victory at Bosworth. There is an unsubstantiated tradition at Eastwell, in Kent, that a member of the royal Plantagenet family lived there in secret who may have been an illegitimate son of Richard III, or indeed, Edward V himself; we shall probably never know the truth.

IMPRISONMENT IN THE TOWER

Edward, and his younger brother Richard, travelled from Ludlow to the Tower of London, which was then the principal royal palace, in May, in preparation for the coronation. Following Edward's declared illegitimacy by parliament, the brothers were probably merely confined to their quarters, rather than being imprisoned in a dungeon.

GOVERNMENT   HEALTH & MEDICINE   JUSTICE   RELIGION   SCIENCE

RICHARD III

BORN 1452 • ACCEDED 1483 • DIED 1485

ichard, Duke of Gloucester, was appointed Protector of England during his nephew, Edward V's, minority. Within two months of Edward's coronation, he was declared illegitimate by Parliament and deposed, whether at the hands of Richard we shall never know, but as Edward IV's legitimate heir he was invited by Parliament to rule as Richard III. Richard is perhaps the most maligned figure in British history, largely as a result of the political propaganda put about by the Tudors following their usurpation of the crown in 1485. Contemporary accounts state that he was close to his brother, Edward IV, and had a kindly disposition. He was tall and considered quite handsome, and was very popular with the people.

COUNCIL OF THE NORTH

Since Norman times the north of England had received somewhat harsher treatment by the monarchy than other regions, partly fuelled by the rebellious nature of the people there who felt that their needs, so far away from the centre of government, were neglected. Richard tried to redress this imbalance by creating the Council of the North, which sought to improve the region's administration.

COLLEGE OF ARMS

The present College of Arms building in London dates from about 1670, but the college itself was founded by Richard III in 1483. The college has its origins in the group of royal retainers known as heralds, whose job it was to carry messages and arrange state occasions. The task of regulating the coats-of-arms of each noble household became part of their duties, which Richard organised into a college.

SHAKESPEARE'S IMAGE

The historical image of Richard is a far cry from the figure portrayed by Shakespeare as a deformed hunchback, a monstrous tyrant and murderer of his two nephews. Shakespeare, who was a royal favourite of his day, based his play on books written by Henry VII's supporters who, in attempting to justify their violent seizure of the crown, created the myth of an evil tyrant that still persists today.

1483
Richard III accedes to the throne after his nephew, Edward V is declared illegitimate and deposed.

1483
Duke of Buckingham leads unsuccessful rebellion against Richard.

1483
Foundation of the College of Arms.
1484
Richard's son, Edward, dies

leaving no heir.
1484
Abolition of Benevolences

🏛 ARCHITECTURE   📖 ARTS & LITERATURE   ⚐ EXPLORATION   💥 FAMOUS BATTLE

BATTLE OF BOSWORTH FIELD

The Battle of Bosworth took place in a field outside the Leicestershire town of Market Bosworth on 22nd August 1485. Henry Tudor's army of between 7-8,000 faced a superior force of about 11-12,000. The battle could have gone either way, but when Richard III himself was killed, his supporters drifted away, leaving the Lancastrian Henry Tudor victor. It brought to a bloody close the dynastic struggle known as the 'Wars of the Roses'.

⚖ THE INTRODUCTION OF BAIL

Richard was actually a wise and very benevolent king, belying his popular image. He introduced a system of bail into court proceedings for defendants, which forms the basis of the system in use today.

📜 PARLIAMENTARY REFORMS

Richard introduced several parliamentary reforms during his short reign, the most significant perhaps being a law passed in 1484 decreeing that all future parliamentary statutes should be written in English and not French or Latin. He also abolished the practice of nobles giving compulsory gifts to the monarchy to win favour.

MIDDLEHAM CASTLE

Sometimes called the 'Windsor of the North', Middleham Castle, in Wensleydale, Yorkshire, was Richard's favourite residence, particularly when touring with the royal court. The present castle dates from about 1170 and contains one of the largest, and grandest, Norman keeps ever built. It passed into the Neville family about a century later. The last Neville to own it was Warwick ('the Kingmaker') and after his death at the Battle of Barnet in 1470 it passed into royal hands. Richard's only son was born and died there.

ANNE NEVILLE

Richard married Anne Neville in 1472. She was the daughter of Richard Neville, Earl of Warwick ('the Kingmaker'). Before Warwick's change of allegiance, their two families had been very close and they were allegedly childhood sweethearts. Middleham Castle, which Richard inherited, had been her childhood home. She died in 1485 shortly before Richard's death in battle at Bosworth.

events individuals selling favour by giving of gifts to royalty.
1484
Council of the

North created to give fairer treatment to those in the north.
1484
Bail introduced into

court system.
1484
English language used in parliamentary acts.
1485
Henry Tudor

lands in West Wales to claim the throne.
1485
Richard's queen, Anne Neville, dies.

1485
Battle of Bosworth - Richard III is defeated and killed, marking an end to the Wars of the Roses.

🖋 GOVERNMENT   🥣 HEALTH & MEDICINE   ⚖ JUSTICE   ✝ RELIGION   𝄃 SCIENCE

WARS OF THE ROSES

(1455~1485)

Although usually described as a civil war, the Wars of the Roses were, more correctly, a dynastic struggle between two families with rival claims to the throne. They were really a series of intermittent battles that took place over a period of 30 years between the private armies of the claimants and did not, essentially, affect the everyday lives of the majority of the population. Both claimants were branches of the same family. Trouble first began when Henry Bolingbroke of Lancaster seized the crown from Richard II in 1399, though it was some years before it lea to outright warfare.

BLOODY BATTLES

The wars began with the Battle of St. Albans in 1455 and ended at the Battle of Bosworth in 1485. There were only 10 major skirmishes between the two sides and the total period of fighting lasted only 13 weeks. Henry VI is shown above having been captured by a subservient Earl of Warwick after the battle of Northampton, 10 July 1460.

THE WHITE ROSE OF YOR

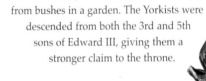

Here, nobles are seen choosing sides in the war by picking eith a red rose (Lancaster) or a white rose (York) from bushes in a garden. The Yorkists were descended from both the 3rd and 5th sons of Edward III, giving them a stronger claim to the throne.

A NEW DYNASTY-THE TUDORS

The Tudor monarchs took their name from Owain Tudor, who claimed descent from the Welsh royal family. Henry Tudor's (later Henry VII) mother was Margaret Beaufort, great-grand-daughter of John of Gaunt, of the House of Lancaster. Once established on the throne, the Tudors set about uniting a divided nation after years of civil unrest. Not always popular, they were noted for their strong government.

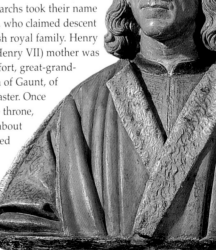

THE WARRIOR KING, HENRY V

Henry V, immortalised as a hero by Shakespeare, ascended the throne in 1413 at the age of 25 and immediately set about regaining his lost French lands. His most famous victory was at Agincourt in 1415, when English archers defeated the might of the French cavalry.

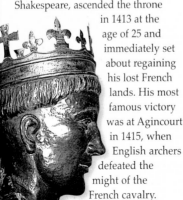

🏛 ARCHITECTURE   📖 ARTS & LITERATURE   ⚐ EXPLORATION   ⬥ FAMOUS BATTLE

THE RED ROSE OF LANCASTER

he Lancastrian claim to the throne was through Henry, Duke of
caster, the son of John of Gaunt, who was the 4th son of Edward III.
The Lancastrians, under Henry Tudor, eventually won the war.

THE FAMILIES UNITED

After his coronation, Henry VII (a Lancastrian)
married Elizabeth of York, daughter of Edward
IV, thus uniting the two families. The Tudor rose
symbolised the new dynasty by incorporating
both red and white roses.

HENRY VI: A WEAK MONARCH

A deeply religious man, Henry was an inept
ruler who lost all of his French lands.
Deposed in 1461 in favour of Edward IV,
he was briefly reinstated in 1470 before
being murdered the following year.

WARWICK: THE KINGMAKER

Richard Neville, Earl of Warwick, was known
as 'the Kingmaker' because he was
instrumental in placing Edward IV on
the throne in 1461. He later engineered
a plot to remove him in 1470.

MY KINGDOM FOR A HORSE

The much-maligned Richard III suffered at
the hands of Tudor propagandists, including
Shakespeare, but history paints him in a
kinder light. He was killed at the Battle
of Bosworth in 1485.

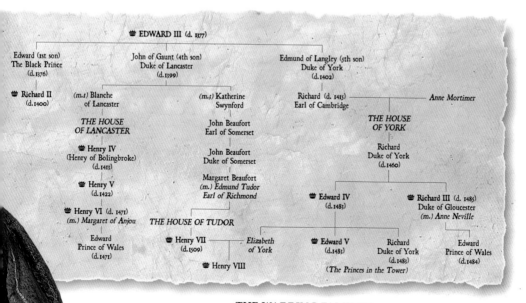

THE WARRING FAMILIES

This family tree shows the relationship of the families contesting the crown. The houses of
Lancaster and York were both branches of the Plantagenet dynasty.

GOVERNMENT   HEALTH & MEDICINE   JUSTICE   RELIGION   SCIENCE

HENRY VII

BORN 1457 • ACCEDED 1485 • DIED 1509

espite the violent way in which he came to the throne, Henry was an advocate of peace and diplomacy; above all he was a businessman. The 'Wars of the Roses' had severe weakened the grip of the nobility and he took advantage of the situation by promoting busines enterprise and encouraging merchants to expar their interests. Under his rule society changed quite radically, casting off many of the feudal ideals in favour of commercial ones. His policie certainly worked and England prospered under his rule. The Tudor period was more than just the name of a new dynasty, it marked the end of the Middle Ages. To establish his own credibility, Henry conducted a very successful 'smear campaign' to blacken the name of Richard III and may himself have been responsible for the murder of Edward V and his brother.

CLAIMANTS TO THE THRONE

For the first few years of Henry's reign he had to put down a number of Yorkist-led rebellions. Lambert Simnel (in 1487) a boy who claimed to be the Earl of Warwick and Perkin Warbeck (in 1492) who claimed to be a son of Edward IV, both led unsuccessful rebellions.

COURT OF THE STAR CHAMBER

The Court of the Star Chamber, first introduced in the 14th century as a means of controlling the power of the nobility, but which had lapsed somewhat, was revived by Henry. His purpose in doing so was two-fold. First, he felt that England must never again be subjected to the futile waste brought about by civil war, so he banned the raising of private armies. Second, he had himself gained the throne by violent means and by controlling the power of the nobility he secured his own position.

A NEW DYNASTY

Henry was the grandson of Owen Tudor, who claimed to be descended from the independent Princes of Wales. His mother was Margaret Beaufort, great-granddaughter of John of Gaun through whom Henry claimed the English throne.

ARTHUR, PRINCE OF WALES

Prince Arthur was the eldest son of Henry VII and had been groomed for kingship. He married Cather of Aragon, the Spanish king's daughter, in an arrang marriage to unite the two countries. Arthur died, prematurely, in 1502, it is said, before the marriage ha been consummated. When Henry died in 1509 the crov passed to his second son, Henry, who also married his dead brother's widow, Catherine, to maintain the alliance.

| 1485 | 1485 | 1486 | Chamber revived. | made in Nuremberg |
| Henry VII becomes first Tudor monarch of England after defeating Richard III at Bosworth. | Henry forms Yeomen of the Guard as a personal bodyguard service to protect him. | Henry marries Elizabeth of York, uniting the houses of Lancaster and York. 1487 Court of the Star | 1487 Revolt led by Lambert Simnel put down. c.1490 First modern globe | 1491 Henry VII invades Fra 1491 Treaty of Etaples, Her agrees to withdraw fr |

 ARCHITECTURE   ARTS & LITERATURE   EXPLORATION   FAMOUS BATTL

CHRISTOPHER COLUMBUS

Christopher Columbus approached Henry for patronage when he embarked upon his voyages of discovery in the 'New World'. Henry was keen to develop business interests outside of war-torn Europe and considered sponsoring Columbus who, in 1492, re-discovered America.

THE NEW WORLD

Unshackled by the old ideals, the Tudor age really was an age of adventure. Henry was keen to patronise anyone who might further England's prosperity by opening up new trade routes. From 1496 on, Henry sponsored John Cabot, a Venetian who had settled in England, and his three sons to seek out new lands, in return for which he demanded one-fifth of any profits.

PEACE AT LAST

Following Henry's victory at Bosworth, there were several attempts on his life. He responded by forming the Yeomen of the Guard, early in 1485, as personal bodyguards in the royal palace. The red livery of their uniforms is still a familiar sight at the Tower of London today. Henry was a great patron of the arts and encouraged the English Renaissance - the 'revival of learning' - among artists and scholars in the relative peace of his reign.

PEMBROKE CASTLE

Henry was born at Pembroke Castle in South Wales, a magnificent Norman stronghold and seat of the Marshals, Earls of Pembroke. He spent 15 years at Pembroke before being forced to flee to Brittany. He returned to Milford Haven in 1485 to claim the English throne.

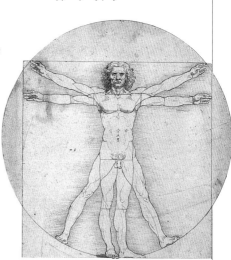

ELIZABETH OF YORK

Within six months of acceding to the throne, Henry (a Lancastrian) married Elizabeth of York, uniting the two warring families and so bringing to an end 30 years of civil war. Despite their obvious political differences it was, by all accounts, a happy marriage and she bore him eight children.

LEONARDO DA VINCI

Leonardo da Vinci (1452-1519) was at the forefront of the Renaissance movement in art and learning. Born in Florence, da Vinci was an artist, an architect and a scientist, whose revolutionary ideas greatly influenced Henry. His most famous work of art is probably the 'Mona Lisa' and the 'Vitruvian Man' is shown above.

...nce in payment of large sum of cash.
1492
erkin Warbeck claims ...rone and leads a revolt against Henry.

1492
Christopher Columbus rediscovers America.
1497
The Cabot brothers sail to North America,

sponsored by Henry.
1499
Perkin Warbeck is executed.
1502
Henry's eldest son, and heir, Prince

Arthur, dies.
1502
First spring-driven watch invented.
1502
Henry's eldest daughter,

Margaret, marries James IV of Scotland, uniting the Tudor and Stuart dynasties.
1509
Henry VII dies.

17

GOVERNMENT   HEALTH & MEDICINE   JUSTICE   RELIGION   SCIENCE

HENRY VIII

BORN 1491 • ACCEDED 1509 • DIED 1547

ILL-HEALTH AND OLD AGE

Henry was plagued by ill-health in later years. He suffered from obesity, severe headaches, smallpox, syphilis, thrombosis and ulcerated legs. He was also grossly overweight and had to be carried up and down stairs using a hoist.

H enry VIII came to the throne at the age of 1 He was a flamboyant character who had n been groomed for kingship and only came to the throne because of the premature death of his elder brother Arthur, in 1502. Well liked at first, he became something of a tyrant in later years, particularly if he did not get his own way. Despite being one of our more well-known monarchs, he was not a great king and is best remembered for breaking with the Church of Rome and for marrying six times.

YOUNG HENRY

As a young man Henry was a robust, athletic man standing 6ft. (1.83 metres) tall. He preferred to spend his time at sports or leisure activities, leaving governance of the country to a group of trusted advisers.

THOMAS WOLSEY

Cardinal Thomas Wolsey (1475-1530) was of humble birth but quickly rose to become one of Henry's most trusted advisers. He was made chancellor in 1514 and virtually governed the country in the early years of Henry's reign, but fell from favour when he failed to secure Henry's divorce from Catherine of Aragon. He was arrested, but died en route to the Tower of London.

MUSICAL PROWESS

Henry VIII was a keen patron of the arts and was himself an accomplished singer and musician. He could play several instruments to quite a high standard, including the harp, organ, virginals (a harpsichord-like instrument) and the lute, shown here. He also composed several tunes including, it is believed, 'Greensleeves'.

1509	brother's widow.	**1515**	**1516**	**1519/22**
Henry VIII succeeds	**1513**	Thomas Wolsey	Queen Catherine gives birth	The Portuguese Ferdin
to the throne.	English defeat	elected Chancellor.	to a girl (later Mary I).	Magellan first person
1509	Scots at Battle	**c.1515**	**1517**	circumnavigate the wo
Henry marries Catherine	of Flodden Field, killing	Coffee first introduced	Martin Luther publishes	**1520**
of Aragon, his dead	James IV.	into Europe.	treatise on anti-Catholicism.	'Field of the Cloth of G

 ARCHITECTURE   **ARTS & LITERATURE**   **EXPLORATION**    **FAMOUS BATTLE**

BATTLE OF FLODDEN FIELD

In 1513 James IV of Scotland invaded northern England in support of the French, with whom Henry was at war. James and many of the Scottish nobility were routed and killed at the Battle of Flodden Field.

✝ MARTIN LUTHER (1483-1546)

Martin Luther was a church reformer from Germany who objected to what he considered corruption within the Catholic Church, for which he was excommunicated. Henry spoke out against Luther's 'Protestant' writings in a book, published in 1521. Ironically, the pope honoured Henry with the title 'Defender of the Faith'. Twelve years later Henry broke with the Church of Rome himself.

PERSECUTIONS

As Henry's reign wore on he became ever more obsessive and tyrannical. removed from office anyone who stood in his way and ordered the executions several thousand people - indeed, one estimate puts the figure as high as 50,000!

THOMAS MORE

Sir Thomas More was Henry's Lord Chancellor and chief minister at the time of his application to annul his marriage to Catherine. He was also a devout Catholic and refused to acknowledge Henry as head of the new English Church following the break with Rome, for which he was executed in 1535, causing a public outcry.

BREAK WITH THE CHURCH OF ROME

There was a growing band of people, called Protestants, who disagreed with many of the Catholic doctrines and who sought church reforms. When the pope refused to annul Henry's marriage to Catherine of Aragon the Protestants seized upon the opportunity to establish a new church and lent their support to the king. Although England eventually broke away from the Church of Rome, Henry himself remained a Catholic. The Church of England did not become fully Protestant until Elizabeth I's reign.

✝ DISSOLUTION OF THE MONASTERIES

By Henry's time many of the monastic ideals had become somewhat lax so, as head of the new Church of England, he seized upon the opportunity to close them down and claim their wealth. Many of the charges levelled against the monks were false, but between 1536-40 Thomas Cromwell, acting as Henry's agent, closed down, or 'dissolved', all of the monasteries, claiming all their lands and possessions for the crown.

🗋 ACT OF SUPREMACY

In 1533 parliament passed the Act of Appeals, which asserted England's independence from the Church of Rome. It was ratified the following year with the Act of Supremacy, which made Henry 'Supreme Head of the Church of England'.

---

peace talks between Henry and France.
1525
William Tyndale ublishes translation of the New Testament.

1529
Cardinal Wolsey accused of high treason, dies whilst awaiting trial.
c.1530
First coalmines in England

open in Newcastle.
1533
Henry's marriage to Catherine of Aragon is annulled by Archbishop Thomas Cranmer.

1533
Henry marries Anne Boleyn.
1533
Anne gives birth to a girl (later Elizabeth I).

1533
Henry is excommunicated.
1534
Act of Supremacy establishes Henry as head of new Church of England.

🏛 GOVERNMENT   🥄 HEALTH & MEDICINE   ⚖ JUSTICE   ✝ RELIGION   🗋 SCIENCE

CATHERINE OF ARAGON

**BORN 1485 • MARRIED 1509
DIVORCED 1533 • DIED 1536**

Catherine of Aragon was the daughter of King Ferdinand of Spain. She was beautiful, intelligent and fun-loving and was betrothed to Henry VII's eldest son Arthur to form an Anglo-Spanish alliance. They married in 1501 but within six months she was widowed. In 1509 she married Henry VIII, initially to keep the alliance but they are said to have genuinely loved one another and remained happily married for 20 years. She gave birth to several children but only one, Princess Mary, survived. It was only after her inability to conceive a son and heir for Henry that he commenced divorce proceedings. He originally tried to have the marriage annulled on the grounds that as his sister-in-law it was an unlawful union. The pope denied Henry so he broke with the Church of Rome and divorced her in 1533. She was banished from court and died three years later.

ANNE BOLEYN

**BORN 1502 • MARRIED 1533 •
DIVORCED 1536 • EXECUTED 153**

When it became clear that Catherine was not going to give him the son he so desperately wanted, Henry began to take several mistresses including the queen's young lady-in-waiting, Anne Boleyn. Henry courted her her family home, Hever Castle, in Kent, and they married in secret in January 1533, four months before his divorce from Catherine was finalised. She gave birth to Princess Elizabeth in September of the same year. When Anne too failed to deliver him a son he commenced divorce proceedings against her als She was accused of adultery with, amongst others, her own brother. The marriage was annulled on 17th May 1536 and two days later Henry had her executed.

JANE SEYMOUR

**BORN 1509 • MARRIED 1536
DIED 1537**

When Anne Boleyn also failed to give Henry a son he began to cast his eye towards her lady-in-waiting, Jane Seymou At first Jane declined his advances and insisted on bein; chaperoned in his presence. They were married just two weeks after Anne Boleyn's execution. In October the followin; year, 1537, Jane gave birth to a son, Edward, by Caesarean section. Complications set in and Jane died of blood poisoning two weeks later. Henry was heartbroken by her death and would probably have remained faithful to her, had she lived.

MARRIAGE STAKES

This timeline (below) shows that although Henry married si× times, over two thirds of his reign was spent with his first wi⨠ Catherine of Aragon. He married all of his other five wives ir the last 11 years of his reign.

YEARS OF MARRIAGE

Catherine of Aragon 24yrs

Anne of Cleves 6months

Anne Boleyn 3yrs

Jane Seymour 1yr

Catherine Howard 2yrs

Catherine Parr 5yrs

1509

154⨠

🏛 ARCHITECTURE   📖 ARTS & LITERATURE   ⮎ EXPLORATION   ✸ FAMOUS BATTLE⨠

THE SIX WIVES OF HENRY VIII

CATHERINE HOWARD

BORN 1521 • MARRIED 1540
EXECUTED 1542

Henry VIII is perhaps best remembered in history for being our most married monarch. He married six times, the first three of which were said to be genuine love matches. The last three were purely political or for reasons of expediency. Henry became obsessed with producing a male heir ('the king's great matter'). He had been happily married to Catherine of Aragon for the first 10 years of his reign and married all of the other five within the last 11 years.

Henry seems to have developed a liking for his current queen's lady-in-waiting. He took an instant liking to Anne of Cleves' lady servant, Catherine Howard, the Duke of Norfolk's niece. She was high-spirited and flirtatious, which at first aroused Henry's interest, but later was the cause of his jealousy. She married Henry just 16 days after the king's divorce from Anne, but less than two years later she was executed, at the young age of 21, accused of adultery, unseemly behaviour and treason.

ANNE OF CLEVES

BORN 1515 • MARRIED 1540
DIVORCED 1540 • DIED 1557

Following Jane Seymour's death Henry might not have married again, especially as he now had the son he had so long craved, but he was placed under mounting political pressure by Thomas Cromwell and other ministers to marry again. Reluctantly he agreed to a marriage of convenience to the German princess, Anne of Cleves, forming an alliance between Germany and England to ward off a threatened Franco-Spanish invasion to re-establish papal power. Henry disliked her intensely, calling her the 'Flanders Mare', and refused to consummate the marriage. They were divorced just six months later.

CATHERINE PARR

BORN 1512 • MARRIED 1543 • DIED 1548

Catherine Parr was a quiet, well-educated lady of comparatively mature years (when she married Henry), in stark contrast to her predecessors. Henry was by that time suffering from several serious ailments and Catherine acted more as a nurse than a wife. Henry was fond of her and appreciated the sense of calm she brought to the royal household. Already twice widowed before marrying Henry, she married again soon after his death, but died the following year during childbirth.

1536 Anne Boleyn accused of adultery and executed.	Jane Seymour. **1537** Queen Jane gives birth to a boy (later Edward VI).	following complications after childbirth. **1540** Henry marries Anne of Cleves, divorces her later the same year.	**1540** Henry marries Catherine Howard.	**1543** Henry marries his sixth wife, Catherine Parr.
1536 Henry marries	**1537** Jane Seymour dies		**1542** Catherine is accused of treason and executed.	**1547** Henry VIII dies.

⚖ GOVERNMENT   🜾 HEALTH & MEDICINE   ⚖ JUSTICE   ✝ RELIGION   🔬 SCIENCE

EDWARD VI

BORN 1537 • ACCEDED 1547 • DIED 1553

& LADY JANE GREY

BORN 1537 • ACCEDED 1553 • DEPOSED 1553 (*9 days later*) • EXECUTED 15

BOY KING

Edward succeeded to the throne at the age of nine. During his minority the country was governed by a Protector. Edward was a sickly child with many of his father's arrogant mannerisms. In January 1553 he contracted tuberculosis and died six months later, aged 15.

GREENWICH PALACE

The Tudor palace of Placentia stood on the banks of the Thames at Greenwich, then a small village in the countryside surrounding London. It was a great favourite of the Tudor monarchs and is where Edward died in 1553. It was rebuilt by Charles II and later extended and converted for use as a naval hospital, college and maritime museum.

dward was the only legitimate son of Henry VIII to survive. Until about the age of five or six he was brought up in the royal nursery, with his half-sister, Elizabeth, but from then on he was groomed for his future role as king by John Cheke. Because his father had remained a Catholic, even after the break with Rome, Edward was the first Protestant monarch of England and under his rule the Reformation of the English Church was consolidated.

THE PROTECTORS

THE DUKE OF SOMERSET

The first Protector appointed to govern during Edward's minority was his uncle, Edward Seymour, Earl of Hertford, later created Duke of Somerset. Unpopular with many of the nobles, he was deposed in 1550 and executed two years later.

THE DUKE OF NORTHUMBERLAND

Following Seymour's deposition, John Dudley, Earl of Warwick, was appointed as Edward's Protector. He created himself Duke of Northumberland and manipulated the young king to suit his own ends. He contrived to marry his son, Lord Guildford Dudley, to Lady Jane Grey and then persuaded the dying Edward (shown here on the day of his coronation) to proclaim Jane queen on his death. When Mary I overthrew Jane and proclaimed herself queen, Northumberland was executed.

1546	1547	an ill-fated plan to	Edward, Seymour,	1549
Henry VIII's last will	*Edward VI accedes*	*place Mary Queen*	*(Duke of Somerset)*	*First Act of Uniformi*
confirms the line of	*to the throne.*	*of Scotts on the*	*becomes Protector*	*bans Roman Catholic m*
succession on his death as	**1547**	*English throne.*	*of England.*	**1549**
Edward, followed by	*English defeat Scots at*	**1547**	**1548**	*First Book of Commo*
Mary, then Elizabeth.	*Battle of Pinkie, as part of*	*Edward's uncle,*	*Catherine Parr dies.*	*Prayer published.*

 ARCHITECTURE   📖 ARTS & LITERATURE   ⚑ EXPLORATION   ◐ FAMOUS BATTLE

A QUEEN FOR NINE DAYS

Lady Jane Grey is one of the tragic figures of English history, an innocent pawn in the often violent and devious power struggles surrounding the line of succession to the throne. She was the Protestant daughter of Frances, Duchess of Suffolk, and Henry VIII's great-niece. An intelligent, quiet and beautiful girl, she became a good friend of Edward, her cousin. When Edward lay on his deathbed he was persuaded by his Protector John Dudley, Duke of Northumberland, to name Jane as his successor to ensure that the throne remained in Protestant hands. Jane reluctantly agreed, but ruled for just nine days, in July 1553, before being taken prisoner by Mary, Edward's half-sister and rightful heir. She was executed the following year when just 17 years old.

LINE OF SUCCESSION

On 30th December 1546 Henry VIII made his last will (right) in which he settled the line of succession. Sensing perhaps that his own death was imminent, he may also have had reservations about the health of his son and made provision for, first Mary and then Elizabeth, to succeed Edward should he die.

📜 ACT OF UNIFORMITY

The Reformation of the church that had been instigated by Henry VIII was consolidated by parliament during Edward's reign, overseen by the king's Protector, Edward Seymour, Duke of Somerset. The first Act of Uniformity was passed in 1549 which banned the Catholic mass and demanded all paintings and idolatry be removed from churches.

✝ BOOK OF COMMON PRAYER

The First Book of Common Prayer was written by Thomas Cranmer (above), Archbishop of Canterbury, and published in 1549. For the first time the mass was read in English instead of Latin, which greatly offended many Catholics who disagreed with the Reformation. Many riots broke out around the country, which were put down by force.

💣 BATTLE OF PINKIE

When Henry VIII died the Scots took the opportunity to try to unite the two countries by forcing Edward to marry his Catholic cousin Mary, Queen of Scots. The English army thwarted the attempt and defeated the Scots at the Battle of Pinkie in 1547.

1549 Church services changed from Latin to English. **1550** Duke of Somerset	deposed and replaced by John Dudley, Earl of Warwick. **1551** Leonard Digges invents the theodolite.	**1552** Duke of Somerset is executed. **1553** Edward contracts tuberculsis.	**1553** Edward VI dies. **1553** Lady Jane Grey is proclaimed queen; she rules for nine days.	**1553** Lady Jane Grey is arrested by Mary I when she accedes to the throne.

📜 GOVERNMENT   🥣 HEALTH & MEDICINE   ⚖️ JUSTICE   ✝ RELIGION   📏 SCIENCE

♱ PROTESTANT BISHOPS EXECUTED

As part of her policy to return England to Catholicism, Mary rescinded all anti-Catholic laws introduced by Edward VI and replaced all of the Protestant bishops. Three of the leading Protestant clergymen, Nicholas Ridley (Bishop of London), Hugh Latimer and Thomas Cranmer (Archbishop of Canterbury) were burnt at the stake for heresy.

SMITHFIELD MARTYRS

Altogether, Mary is believed to have had nearly 300 Protestants executed. The largest mass execution, and the one which so repulsed the population, was at Smithfield in London, in 1555, when 43 martyrs were burnt at the stake. Excavations in 1849, near St. Bartholomew's Hospital, revealed charred oak posts and human remains. A memorial was set up at the hospital.

RESTORATION OF CATHOLICISM

Although she had been forced to acknowledge her parents' divorce and sign the oath of succession, Mary wrote secretly to the pope stating that she was forced to do so and would revert the country to Catholicism should she ever accede to the throne. She revived the laws of heresy but many refused to acknowledge papal authority. She excused her cruel behaviour by saying that it was necessary to save their souls from the evil of Protestantism.

MARRIAGE TO PHILIP OF SPAIN

Mary married Philip of Spain in July 1554, partly to form an alliance with Spain and partly to strengthen the return to Catholicism, but it was an unhappy marriage and produced no children. Philip spent hardly any time with her in England and when he succeeded to the Spanish throne in 1556 he left England and never returned.

1553
Lady Jane Grey is proclaimed Protestant successor by the Protector, the Duke of Northumberland,

but she is arrested and imprisoned by Mary 9 days later.
1553
Mary I accedes to the throne on

the death of her younger brother, Edward VI.
1554
Mary marries the Catholic, Philip of Spain.

1554
Sir Thomas Wyatt leads rebellion against Mary's marriage to Philip of Spain.

1554
Wyatt and Lady Jane Grey executed.
1554
Mary reverts England to Catholicism.

🏛 ARCHITECTURE   📖 ARTS & LITERATURE   ⚐ EXPLORATION   ⬤ FAMOUS BATTLES

MARY I

BORN 1516 • ACCEDED 1553 • DIED 1558

Mary I was probably one of our most unpopular monarchs. She was the daughter of Henry VIII by his first wife, Catherine of Aragon, a Spaniard, and was brought up a devout Catholic. She became embittered when her parents were divorced and her accession to the throne was denied. When Edward VI died in 1553 she was again passed over in favour of Lady Jane Grey. Not to be denied this time, however, she marched on London and deposed Jane.

LOSS OF CALAIS

In 1557 Mary declared war on France, but it was short-lived. The following year the French successfully took Calais, the last remaining English possession in France.

WYATT'S REBELLION

Many people objected to Mary's marriage and at having a Catholic foreigner sharing the English throne. Sir Thomas Wyatt, Sheriff of Kent, led a rebellion in protest at the marriage in 1554. He had initial success, defeating a royal army at Strood and capturing Cooling Castle, in Kent, but the rebellion was badly organised and later collapsed. Wyatt was executed at the Tower of London for treason.

'BLOODY MARY'

A bitter, morose woman, Mary frequently incurred the wrath of Henry VIII and refused to acknowledge her half-sister, Princess Elizabeth.

Under her rule Protestants were cruelly persecuted and many were burned at the stake for heresy, earning her the title, 'Bloody Mary'.

CARDINAL REGINALD POLE

Cardinal Reginald Pole, a loyal and faithful Catholic, was appointed Archbishop of Canterbury in 1556 after the Protestant bishops had been deposed. His intention was to reverse all of the recent church reforms and restore the pope as supreme head of the church in England. However, he died shortly after Mary in 1558 before many of his policies could be implemented.

1554-58
Persecution of Protestants with the revival of heresy laws.
1555
Three Protestant bishops burned at the stake for heresy.
1556
Cranmer, former Archbishop of Canterbury, executed.
1556
Cardinal Reginald Pole is appointed Archbishop of Canterbury.
1556
Philip becomes king of Spain; leaves England.
1557
England declares war with France.
1558
England loses Calais, last possession in France.
1558
Mary I dies, childless.

🏛 GOVERNMENT   ⚕ HEALTH & MEDICINE   ⚖ JUSTICE   ✝ RELIGION   ▯ SCIENCE

ELIZABETH I

BORN 1533 • ACCEDED 1558 • DIED 1603

The daughter of Henry VIII and Anne Boleyn, Elizabeth could never have expected to become queen. Third in line to the throne, she spent much of her early life at Hatfield House in Hertfordshire. In 1554 she was briefly imprisoned in the Tower of London because of her suspected involvement in Thomas Wyatt's rebellion.

Although she was a Protestant, she diluted many of the extremes of the church reform to make them more acceptable. She came to the throne at age 25 and was successful in uniting a bitterly divided country. Her reign is marked by its stability. It was an age of adventure and discovery and England prospered as never before, laying the foundations of the British Empire.

THE VIRGIN QUEEN

Elizabeth never married, despite being courted by several very eligible suitors, including Robert Dudley, Earl of Leicester, and Robert Devereux, 2nd Earl of Essex. She chose instead to remain a virgin and devote her life to governing the country. She once said that she was married to the 'Kingdom of England'.

THE BARD OF AVON

William Shakespeare (1564-1616) was at the forefront of the English Renaissance in art and literature. Best known as a playwright, he began his career first as a stage-hand and then as an actor in the theatre. He sometimes gave personal readings of his plays to Elizabeth in her private chambers.

EARL OF ESSEX

Robert Devereux, Second Earl of Essex, was another of Elizabeth's favourites. Although 34 years her junior the queen is said to have genuinely loved him. He used his position at court to further his political career. He betrayed her trust, however, and was executed for treason in 1601.

EARL OF LEICESTER

Robert Dudley, Earl of Leicester, was one of Elizabeth's favourites at court. He entertained her at Kenilworth Castle in 1575 for 19 days and once asked for her hand in marriage, but she refused him.

1558
Elizabeth I accedes to the throne.
1559
Act of Supremacy restores Protestantism and establishes Elizabeth as head of Church of England.
1562
Francis Drake makes first slave-trading voyage to America.

1564
Birth of William Shakespeare.
1568
Mary Queen of Scots flees to England in exile; imprisoned by Elizabeth.
1577/80
Francis Drake completes first circumnavigation of the world by an Englishman.

1580
Elizabeth excommunicated by the pope.
1583
John Somerville attempts to assassinate Elizabeth.

 ARCHITECTURE   ARTS & LITERATURE   EXPLORATION   FAMOUS BATTLES

DRAKE'S CIRCUMNAVIGATION

Francis Drake circumnavigated the world between 1577-80, the first Englishman to do so. On his return he was greeted with a hero's welcome and was knighted by Elizabeth aboard his ship, the 'Golden Hind' (shown left).

ACT OF SUPREMACY

A further Act of Supremacy, passed in 1559, re-established the monarchy as Supreme Head of the Church in England, following Mary's attempts to re-establish papal authority in England.

THE SPANISH ARMADA

Spain sent a massive armada in 1588 as the first stage in a proposed invasion of England. The daring seamanship of Drake, Frobisher, Hawkins and others outmanoeuvred the Spanish fleet, which was routed in a week-long running battle in the Channel. Of 138 ships that set out from Spain, only 67 returned, escaping only by sailing north, around the coasts of Scotland and Ireland.

WALTER RALEIGH

Sir Walter Raleigh, like Drake, Frobisher and other seafaring adventurers, opened up new trade routes in the unexplored regions of the world, bringing home untold riches and exotic goods, such as potatoes, chillies (below) and tobacco. He fell from favour under James I, however, and was executed for treason in 1618.

POOR LAW

In 1601 a Poor Law was passed in Parliament which imposed a poor relief rate on the wealthy to help keep those who could not work because they were blind, sick or crippled. Those who were capable of work, but chose to live as vagabonds, were punished. Poor people receiving relief had to stay within their own parish.

MARY QUEEN OF SCOTS

The Tudors were related to the Stuarts, royal family of Scotland. Elizabeth's cousin Mary, a Catholic and queen of Scotland, was involved in a plot to place her on the English throne. Aware that Mary had been implicated against her will, Elizabeth was reluctant to sign her death warrant, which she did, eventually, after 19 years of imprisonment, in 1587. Elizabeth never married and when she died in 1603 the throne passed to Mary's son, James VI of Scotland (James I of England) as her closest relative.

WAR WITH SPAIN

Ever since Henry VIII's break with the Church of Rome, England was placed under threat of invasion from the Catholic countries of Europe to re-establish papal authority. Elizabeth had refused Philip II's (her brother-in-law) hand in marriage and, as the most powerful country in Europe at that time, Spain needed little encouragement to lead the proposed invasion. Elizabeth gave her permission for her sea captains to perform acts of piracy against Spanish ships, further antagonising Philip. They preyed successfully on the slow and cumbersome galleons, an example of which is shown here.

1587 Mary Queen of Scots is executed. **1588** Spanish Armada defeated	**1592** John David discovers the Falkland Islands, off the Argentinean coast. **1595** Sir Walter Raleigh makes his	first trip to South America. **1596** Sir Francis Drake dies of dysentery in the Caribbean. **1597** Second Spanish Armada	leaves for England, but is scattered by bad weather. **1599** The Edict of Nantes in France grants freedom to Protestants.	**1601** Robert Devereux, Earl of Essex, executed. **1603** Elizabeth I dies; last Tudor monarch.

SCOTTISH KINGS & QUEENS

(1214~1329)

Ever since William I's invasion of Scotland in 1071, when Malcolm III swore fealty to him as overlord, Scotland had fiercely fought for independence from England. In 1189 Richard I gave Scotland its freedom in return for a large cash payment to help fund his crusade to the Holy Land and in 1217 a peace treaty was signed between England and Scotland acknowledging Scotland's independence. Matters came to a head again in 1290 when the infant Margaret, the Maid of Norway and successor to the Scottish throne, died unexpectedly, opening the way for Edward I of England to re-assert his claim to Scotland.

ALEXANDER II
(1214-49)

When Alexander II ascended the Scottish throne in 1214 he was determined to rid the land of Viking invaders. Following several minor successes, in 1249 he tried an all-out assault, but died before the attack could be launched.

LINE OF SUCCESSION

Alexander II - 1214-49
Alexander III - 1249-86
Margaret of Norway - 1286-90
John Balliol - 1292-96
(Edward I of England ruled as king) 1296-1306
Robert I (Bruce) - 1306-29

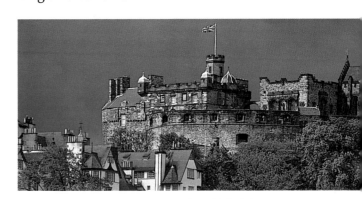

EDINBURGH CASTLE

Edinburgh Castle, home of the Scottish kings, towers 300ft. above the city. Castle Rock has been fortified since at least Iron Age times, though the medieval castle dates from about 1100. When Robert Bruce captured the castle from the English in 1313 he is said to have destroyed every building except the chapel. The castle, which has been largely rebuilt since then, contains part of the Scottish royal palace within its walls.

🏛 ARCHITECTURE   📖 ARTS & LITERATURE   ⚑ EXPLORATION   🜂 FAMOUS BATTLE

BATTLE OF BANNOCKBURN

...is decisive battle between Scotland, under Robert Bruce, and ...ngland, under Edward II, took place near Stirling Castle on 23rd-24th June 1314. The Scots emerged victorious.

THE STONE OF SCONE

...cottish monarchs were traditionally enthroned on this stone. In 1296 it ...vas removed from Scone Abbey by Edward I to Westminster. It was returned in 1996 and can now be seen in Edinburgh Castle.

ALEXANDER III (1249-86)

...lexander III ascended the throne at just eight years old in 1249. He defeated the Vikings in 1263 and proved to be an able administrator. He died in an accident in 1286.

JOHN BALLIOL (1292-96)

In 1290 the Scottish throne fell vacant. A successor could not be ...greed so Edward I of England was asked to mediate. He chose John Balliol, a weak man whom he thought he could manipulate.

WILLIAM WALLACE

In 1295 John Balliol formed an alliance with France against England. The following year Edward I invaded Scotland, deposed Balliol and proclaimed himself King of Scotland. The Scots rebelled, led by William Wallace, who defeated Edward at the Battle of Stirling Bridge. In 1298 Edward re-invaded Scotland and defeated Wallace at the Battle of Falkirk. Wallace continued to lead the revolt against England until 1305, when he was betrayed and captured. He was found guilty of treason and was hanged, drawn and quartered.

ROBERT BRUCE (1306-29)

Following the execution of William Wallace in London, Robert Bruce declared himself leader of the rebels against English rule, even though he had originally offered his support to Edward. He was crowned King of Scotland as Robert I in 1306. The following year Edward re-invaded Scotland. Edward died en route but his invasion army forced Bruce into hiding. Bruce gradually gathered his strength and attacked Stirling Castle in 1314. Even after the English were defeated at Bannockburn, Scotland did not gain full independence. Bruce invaded England in 1327 and the following year Edward III signed the Treaty of Edinburgh, finally acknowledging Scotland's independence. Bruce died a year later.

GOVERNMENT · HEALTH & MEDICINE · JUSTICE · RELIGION · SCIENCE

💧 BATTLE OF OTTERBURN

Richard II, of England, was a far less able king than his predecessor Edward III had been and in the border struggles between England and Scotland of the 14th century Scotland gained the upper hand. In 1388 Robert II defeated the English at the Battle of Otterburn.

ROBERT III (1390-1406)

When Robert II died the throne passed to his son John, who was crowned as Robert III. Curiously, although he had largely governed the country during his father's reign, when he himself became king he relinquished much of his power to his younger brother, Alexander. It was a period of excessive violence and near anarchy, when the Scottish monarchy turned to France yet again as an ally in its wars with England.

TREATY OF BERWICK

In 1346 David II invaded England but was defeated at Neville's Cross and confined to the Tower of London for 11 years. He was finally released in 1357 on signing the Treaty of Berwick in which he agreed to pay a huge ransom to Edward III of England, payable by instalments. Unable to make his payments, in 1363 David offered his throne to Edward III if he agreed to cancel the debt, but the Scottish parliament refused to sanction such a deal, stating that they would prefer to bankrupt the country rather than give in to such treachery by David.

LINE OF SUCCESSION

David II (Bruce) - 1329-32 & 1341-71
Edward Balliol - 1332-41
Robert II - 1371-90
Robert III - 1390-1406

EDWARD BALLIOL (1332-41)

In 1332 John Balliol's son, Edward, entered into an alliance with Edward III, of England. David II was driven into exile and Edward was crowned king, but on condition that he handed over large tracts of lowland Scotland to the English king. In 1341 Balliol was overthrown and David II re-asserted his claim to the throne.

SCOTTISH KINGS & QUEENS

1329 ~ 1406

The 14th century was a period of almost constant struggle in Scotland to maintain the right for independence. The border counties of both England and Scotland were often the scene of bloody skirmishes as each struggled for supremacy and the land often changed hands between the two countries. Scotland formed an uneasy alliance with France, England's age-old enemy, in its bid for independence, though the French were frequently far from happy with the situation, which often worked against their own plans. It was a period of social unrest, weak governance and violence as the Scottish lords also struggled among themselves for supremacy.

DAVID II (1329-32 & 1341-71)

Following the bitter struggles of Robert Bruce's reign to maintain Scottish independence, the reign of his son, David II, was a complete disappointment to the people of Scotland. Although a long reign, his rule was marked by weakness and treachery; he even tried to sell his sovereignty to Edward III of England.

CAPTURE OF PRINCE JAMES

In 1406 Henry IV of England captured the 12 year old Prince James, Robert III's son, and imprisoned him in the Tower of London. The news is said to have brought on Robert's premature death. James remained a prisoner for 18 years, Scotland being ruled by his uncle, the Duke of Albany, in his absence.

ROBERT II (1371-90)

When David II died in 1371 he was succeeded by his nephew, Robert Stewart (or Stuart). He was the High Steward of Scotland and Robert Bruce's grandson. He was also the first Stuart monarch, so beginning a new Scottish dynasty, though he was a weak king and left much of the business of government to his eldest son, John, Earl of Carrick.

GOVERNMENT   HEALTH & MEDICINE   JUSTICE   RELIGION   SCIENCE

THE HOUSE OF LANCASTER, YORK & THE TUDORS

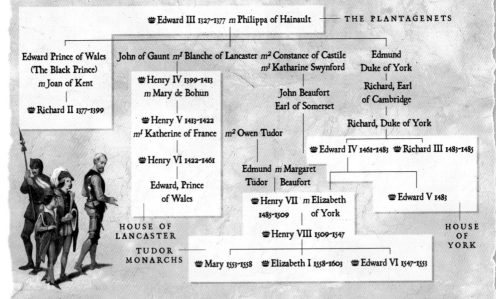

♛ Edward III 1327-1377 *m* Philippa of Hainault — THE PLANTAGENETS

Edward Prince of Wales
(The Black Prince)
m Joan of Kent

♛ Richard II 1377-1399

John of Gaunt *m¹* Blanche of Lancaster *m²* Constance of Castile
m³ Katharine Swynford

♛ Henry IV 1399-1413
m Mary de Bohun

♛ Henry V 1413-1422
m¹ Katherine of France *m²* Owen Tudor

♛ Henry VI 1422-1461

Edward, Prince
of Wales

Edmund
Duke of York

Richard, Earl
of Cambridge

John Beaufort
Earl of Somerset

Richard, Duke of York

♛ Edward IV 1461-1483   ♛ Richard III 1483-1485

Edmund *m* Margaret
Tudor | Beaufort

♛ Henry VII *m* Elizabeth
1485-1509   of York

♛ Henry VIII 1509-1547

♛ Edward V 1483

HOUSE OF
LANCASTER

TUDOR
MONARCHS

HOUSE
OF
YORK

♛ Mary 1553-1558   ♛ Elizabeth I 1558-1603   ♛ Edward VI 1547-1553

Both the Houses of Lancaster and York were separate branches of the Plantagenet dynasty and each claimed the throne of England. The dispute eventually led to the Wars of the Roses. The struggle finally came to an end in 1485 when Henry Tudor, who claimed descent from the independent princes of Wales, defeated and killed Richard III in battle in 1485. His mother was descended from the House of Lancaster, from whom Henry claimed the English throne.

ACKNOWLEDGEMENTS

This Series is dedicated to J. Allan Twiggs whose enthusiasm for British History has inspired these four books.
We would also like to thank: Graham Rich, Tracey Pennington, and Peter Done for their assistance.
ticktock Publishing Ltd., The Offices in the Square, Hadlow, Kent TN11 ODD, UK
A CIP Catalogue for this book is available from the British Library. ISBN 1 86007 019 1

Acknowledgements: Picture Credits t=top, b=bottom, c=centre, l=left, r=right, OFC=outside front cover, IFC=inside front cover, IBC=inside back cover, OBC=outside back cover.

AKG, London: 17cr (Galleria dell' Accademia Florence) & OBC. Ancient Art & Architecture: 2tl, 3t, 5r & inset, 7bl (detail), 7t, 8tl, 11tl & tr, 13t, 14bl, 17t, 19tl, 24tr, 25t & b. Bridgeman Art Library: OFC, 3r (detail), 4, 5t & IFC, 8b (detail), 9t & OBC, 9br, 10cl (detail), 12tl & OBC (detail), 14tl (detail), br, 15t, 16tl, 20tr &cr, 21cl, 23tl & cr, 30 tr & OBC (detail). Mary Evans Picture Library: 6l, 9bl, 10br & tl (detail) & 32 tl, 12br, 16bc, 18cl, 19br, 20l, 22br, 26tl, 27t, 30l, 30br, 31tr & br. Chris Fairclough / Image Select: 2c, 7br, 13c, 17cl & OBC, 28b. Glasgow Museums : The Stirling Maxwell Collection: 24. Hever Castle Ltd: 18cr. Hulton Getty Collection: 23br, 28tl. National Gallery (Scotland): 29bc & OFC. National Maritime Museum (London): 26 cr & OFC. Board of Trustees of the National Museums and Galleries on Merseyside (Walker Art Gallery, Liverpool): OFC. National Portrait Gallery (London): 18tl, 21tr & br. Spectrum Colour Library: 29tr. The Master and Fellows of Corpus Christie College Cambridge: 29tl

Every effort has been made to trace the copyright holders and we apologise in advance for any unintentional omissions. We would be pleased to insert the appropriate acknowledgement in any subsequent edition of this publication.

Printed in Italy

A 1,000 YEARS OF BRITISH HISTORY - THE MILLENNIUM SERIES

BOOK I (1,000~1399)   BOOK II (1399~1603)   BOOK III (1603~1714)   BOOK IV (1714~ present day)